# The Sermons of Mr. Yorick

Anonymous

Copyright © BiblioLife, LLC

This book represents a historical reproduction of a work originally published before 1923 that is part of a unique project which provides opportunities for readers, educators and researchers by bringing hard-to-find original publications back into print at reasonable prices. Because this and other works are culturally important, we have made them available as part of our commitment to protecting, preserving and promoting the world's literature. These books are in the "public domain" and were digitized and made available in cooperation with libraries, archives, and open source initiatives around the world dedicated to this important mission.

We believe that when we undertake the difficult task of re-creating these works as attractive, readable and affordable books, we further the goal of sharing these works with a global audience, and preserving a vanishing wealth of human knowledge.

Many historical books were originally published in small fonts, which can make them very difficult to read. Accordingly, in order to improve the reading experience of these books, we have created "enlarged print" versions of our books. Because of font size variation in the original books, some of these may not technically qualify as "large print" books, as that term is generally defined; however, we believe these versions provide an overall improved reading experience for many.

# THE
# SERMONS
## OF
## Mr. YORICK.

### VOL. IV.

A NEW EDITION.

LONDON:
Printed for W. STRAHAN; T. BECKET, and
T. CADELL, in the Strand.
MDCCLXXVI.

# CONTENTS OF THE FOURTH VOLUME.

### SERMON VIII.
The Parable of the rich Man and Lazarus.

### SERMON IX.
Pride.

### SERMON X.
Humility.

### SERMON XI.
Advantages of Chriſtianity to the World.

# CONTENTS.

## SERMON XII.
The abuses of Conscience considered.

## SERMON XIII.
Temporal Advantages of Religion.

## SERMON XIV.
Our Conversation in Heaven.

# SERMON VIII.

The Parable of the RICH MAN and LAZARUS confidered.

### LUKE xvi. 31.

*And he faid unto him, If they hear not Mofes and the prophets, neither will they be perfuaded, though one fhould rife from the dead.*

THESE words are the conclufion of the parable of the rich man and Lazarus; the defign of which was to fhew us the neceffity of conducting ourfelves, by fuch lights as God had been pleafed to give us: the fenfe and meaning of the patriarch's final determination in the text being this, That they who will not be perſuaded to anſwer the great purpoſes of their being, upon ſuch arguments as are offered to them in ſcripture, will never be perſuaded to it by any other means, how extraordinary ſoever;—*If they hear not Moſes and the prophets, neither will they be perſuaded, though one ſhould riſe from the dead*———

———Riſe from the dead! To what purpoſe? What could ſuch a meſſenger propoſe or urge, which had not been propoſed and urged already? the novelty or ſurpriſe of ſuch a viſit might awaken the attention of a curious unthinking people, who ſpent their time in nothing elſe, but to hear and tell ſome new thing; but ere the wonder was well over, ſome new won-

## SERMON VIII.

der would start up in its room, and then the man might return to the dead from whence he came, and not a soul make one inquiry about him.

―― This, I fear, would be the conclusion of the affair. But to bring this matter still closer to us, let us imagine, if there is nothing unworthy in it, that God, in compliance with a curious world,――or from a better motive,――in compassion to a sinful one, should vouchsafe to send one from the dead, to call home our conscience and make us better Christians, better citizens, better men, and better servants to God than what we are.

Now bear with me, I beseech you, in framing such an address, as I imagine, would be most likely to gain our attention, and conciliate the heart to what he had to say: the great channel to it, is Interest,——and there he would set out.

He might tell us, (after the most indisputable credentials of whom he served) That he was come a messenger from the great God of Heaven, with reiterated proposals, whereby much was to be granted us on his side,——and something to be parted with on ours: but that, not to alarm us,——'twas neither houses, nor land, nor possessions;—'twas neither wives, or children, or brethren, or sisters, which we had to forsake;——no one rational pleasure to be given up;——no natural endearment to be torn from——

## SERMON VIII.

———In a word, he would tell us, We had nothing to part with———but what was not for our interests to keep,———and that was our Vices; which brought death and misery to our doors.

He would go on, and prove it by a thousand arguments, that to be temperate and chaste, and just and peaceable, and charitable and kind to one another,———was only doing that for CHRIST's sake, which was most for our own; and that were we in a capacity of capitulating with GOD upon what terms we would submit to his government,———he would convince us, 'twould be impossible for the wit of man to frame any proposals more for our present interests, than *to lead an uncorrupted life——to do the thing which is lawful and right*, and lay such restraints upon our appetites as are for the honour of human nature, and the refinement of human happiness.

When this point was made out, and the alarms from Interest got over,——the spectre might address himself to the other passions——in doing this, he could but give us the most engaging ideas of the perfections of God,——or could he do more, than impress the most aweful ones, of his majesty and power:——he might remind us, that we are creatures but of a day, hastening to the place from whence we shall not return;——that during our stay, we stood accountable to this Being, who, tho' rich in mercies,——yet was terrible in his judgments;——that he took notice of all our actions;——that he was about our paths, and about our beds, and spied out all our ways; and was so pure in his nature, that he would punish even the wicked imaginations of the heart, and had appointed a day, wherein he would enter into this inquiry.———

He might add————

But what?——with all the eloquence of an inspired tongue, What could he add or say to us, which has not been said before? The experiment has been tried a thousand times upon the hopes and fears, the reasons and passions of men, by all the powers of nature————

the application of which have been so great, and the variety of addresses so unanswerable, that there is not a greater paradox in the world, than that so good a religion should be no better recommended by its professors.

The fact is, mankind are not always in a humour to be convinced,—and so long as the pre-engagement with our passions subsists, it is not argumentation which can do the business;—we may amuse ourselves with the ceremony of the operation, but we reason not with the proper faculty, when we see every thing in the shape and colouring, in which the treachery of the senses paint it: and indeed, were we only to look into the world, and observe how inclinable men are to defend evil, as well as to commit it, ——one would think, at first sight, they believed, that all discourses of religion and virtue were mere matters of speculation, for men to entertain some idle hours with; and conclude very naturally, that we seemed to be agreed in no one thing, but speaking well,—and acting ill. But the truest comment is in the text,—*If they hear not Moses and the prophets*, &c.

If they are not brought over to the interests of religion upon such discoveries as GOD has made——or has enabled them to make, they will stand out against all evidence:——in vain shall *one* rise for their conviction;—— was the earth to give up her dead—

'twould be the same;————every man would return again to his course, and the same bad passions would produce the same bad actions to the end of the world.

This is the principal lesson of the parable; but I must enlarge upon the whole of it————because it has some other useful lessons, and they will best present themselves to us as we go along.

In this parable, which is one of the most remarkable in the gospel, our Saviour represents a scene, in which, by a kind of contrast, two of the most opposite conditions that could be brought together from human life, are pass'd before our imaginations.

The one, a man exalted above the level of mankind, to the higheſt pinnacle of proſperity,——to riches——to happineſs——I ſay, *happineſs*,——in compliance with the world, and on a ſuppoſition, that the poſſeſſion of riches muſt make us happy, when the very purſuit of them ſo warms our imagination, that we ſtake both body and ſoul upon the event, as if they were things not to be purchaſed at too dear a rate. They are the wages of wiſdom,——as well as of folly.——Whatever was the caſe here, is beyond the purport of the parable——the ſcripture is ſilent, and ſo ſhould we; it marks only his outward condition, by the common appendages of it, in the two great articles of Vanity and

Appetite:———to gratify the one, he was clothed in purple and fine linen: to satisfy the other,———fared sumptuously every day;———and upon every thing too———we'll suppose, that climates could furnish———that luxury could invent, or the hand of science could torture.

Close by his gates is represented an object whom Providence might seem to have placed there, to cure the pride of man, and shew him to what wretchedness his condition might be brought: a creature in all the shipwreck of nature,———helpless,——undone,———in want of friends, in want of health,———and in want of every thing with them which his distresses called for.

In this state he is described as desiring to be fed with the crumbs which fell from the rich man's table; and tho' the case is not expresſly put, that he was refused; yet as the contrary is not affirmed in the historical part of the parable,———or pleaded after by the other, that he shewed mercy to the miserable, we may conclude his requeſt was unſuccesſful———like too many others in the world, either so high lifted up in it, that they cannot look down diſtinctly enough upon the sufferings of their fellow-creatures, ———or by long surfeiting in a continual course of banqueting and good cheer, they forget there is such a diſtemper as hunger, in the catalogue of human infirmities.

Overcharged with this, and perhaps a thousand unpitied wants in a pilgrimage through an inhospitable world, the poor man sinks silently under his burden.—But, good God! whence is this? Why dost thou suffer these hardships in a world which thou hast made? Is it for thy honour, that one man should eat the bread of fulness, and so many of his own stock and lineage eat the bread of sorrow?——— That this man should go clad in purple, and have all his paths strewed with rosebuds of delight, whilst so many mournful passengers go heavily along, and pass by his gates, hanging down their heads? Is it for thy Glory, O God! that so large a shade of misery should be spread across thy works?———or, Is it that we see but a part of them? When the great chain at length is let down, and all that has held the two worlds in harmony is seen;———when the dawn of that day approaches, in which all the distressful incidents of this Drama shall be unravel'd;———when every man's case shall be reconsidered,———then wilt thou be fully justified in all thy ways, and every mouth shall be stopped.

After a long day of mercy, misspent in riot and uncharitableness, the rich man *died also:*———the parable adds,—and was buried;———Buried no doubt in triumph, with all the ill-timed pride of funerals, and empty decorations, which worldly folly is apt to prostitute upon those occasions.

But this was the last vain show; the utter conclusion of all his epicurean grandeur;——the next is a scene of horror, where he is represented by our Saviour, in a state of the utmost misery, from whence he is supposed to lift up his eyes towards heaven, and cry to the patriarch Abraham for mercy.

*And Abraham said, Son, remember that thou in thy life-time receivedst thy good things.*

——That he had received his good things,—'twas from heaven,——and could be no reproach: with what severity soever the scripture speaks against riches, it does not appear, that the living or faring sumptuously every day, was the crime objected to the rich man; or that it is a real part of a vicious character: the case might be then, as now: his quality and station in the world might be supposed to be such, as not only to have justified his doing this, but, in general, to have required it without any imputation of doing wrong; for differences of stations there must be in the world, which must be supported by such marks of distinction as custom imposes. The exceeding great plenty and magnificence, in which Solomon is described to have lived, who had ten fat oxen, and twenty oxen out of the pastures, and a hundred sheep, besides harts and roebucks, and fallow deer, and fatted fowl, with thirty measures of fine flower, and three-score measures of meal, for the daily provision of his table;——all this is not laid to him as a sin, but rather remarked as an instance of God's blessing to him;——and whenever these things are otherwise, 'tis from a wasteful and dishonest perversion of them to pernicious ends,——and oft-times, to the very opposite ones for which they were granted,——to glad the heart, to open it, and render it more kind.———

And this seems to have been the snare the rich man had fallen into—and possibly, had he fared less sumptuously,——he might have had more cool hours for reflection, and been

## SERMON VIII.

better difpofed to have conceived an idea of want, and to have felt compaffion for it.

*And Abraham faid, Son, remember that thou in thy life time receivedſt thy good things, and likewiſe Lazarus evil things.*——Remember! fad fubject of recollection! that a man has paffed through this world with all the bleſſings and advantages of it, on his fide, ——favoured by GOD Almighty with riches——befriended by his fellow-creatures in the means of acquiring them,——affifted every hour by the fociety of which he is a member, in the enjoyment of them—to remember, how much he has received,—— how little he has beftowed,——that he has been no man's friend,—no one's protector,——no one's benefactor,——bleſſed God!———

Thus begging in vain for himſelf, he is repreſented at laſt as interceding for his brethren, that Lazarus might be ſent to them to give them warning, and ſave them from the ruin which he had fallen into;——*They have Moſes and the prophets,* was the anſwer of the patriarch,——*let them hear them;* but the unhappy man is repreſented, as diſcontented with it; and ſtill perſiſting in his requeſt, and urging,— *Nay, father Abraham, but if one went from the dead, they would repent.*

——He thought ſo——but Abraham knew otherwiſe:——And the grounds of the determination, I have explained already,——ſo ſhall proceed to draw some other conclusions and lessons from the parable.

And first, our SAVIOUR might further intend to discover to us by it, the dangers to which great riches naturally expose mankind, agreeably to what is elsewhere declared, how hardly shall they who have them, enter into the kingdom of Heaven.

The truth is, they are often too dangerous a blessing for GOD to trust us with, or we to manage: they surround us at all times with ease, with nonsense, with flattery, and false friends, with which thousands and ten thousands have perished:——they are apt to multiply our faults, and treacherously to conceal them from us;—— they hourly administer to our temptations;——and neither allow us time to examine our faults, or humility to repent of them:—nay, what is strange, do they not often tempt men even to covetousness? and tho' amidst all the ill offices which riches do us, one would last suspect this vice, but rather think the one a cure for the other; yet so it is, that many a man contracts his spirits upon the enlargement of his fortune, and is the more empty for being full.

But there is less need to preach against this: we seem all to be hastening to the opposite extreme of luxury and expence: we generally content ourselves with the solution of it; and say, 'Tis a natural consequence of trade and riches—and there it ends.

By the way, I affirm, there is a mistake in the account; and that it is not riches which are the cause of luxury,—but the corrupt calculation of the world, in making riches the balance for honour, for virtue, and for every thing that is great and good, which goads so many thousands on with an affectation of possessing more than they have,——and consequently of engaging in a system of expences they cannot support.

In one word, 'tis the necessity of *appearing* to be somebody, in order to be so——which ruins the world.

This leads us to another lesson in the parable, concerning the true use and application of riches; we may be sure from the treatment of the rich man, that he did not employ those talents as God intended.——

How God did intend them,—may as well be known from an appeal to your own hearts, and the inscription you shall read there,——as from any chapter and verse I might cite upon the subject. Let us then for a moment, my dear auditors! turn our eyes that way, and consider the traces which even the most insensible man may have proof of, from what he may perceive springing up within him from some casual act of generosity; and tho' this is a pleasure which properly belongs to the good, yet let him try the experiment;——let him comfort the captive, or cover the naked with a garment, and he will feel what is meant by that moral delight arising in the mind from the conscience of a humane action.

But to know it right, we must call upon the compassionate;——Cruelty gives evidence unwillingly, and feels the pleasure but imperfectly; for this, like all other pleasures, is of a relative nature, and consequently the enjoyment of it, requires some qualification in the faculty, as much as the enjoyment of any other good does:— there must be something antecedent in the disposition and temper which will render that good,——a good to that individual; otherwise, tho' 'tis true it may be possessed,——yet it never can be enjoyed.

Consider how difficult you would find it to convince a miserly heart, that any thing is good, which is not profitable? or a libertine one, that any thing is bad, which is pleasant?

Preach to a voluptuary, who has modell'd both mind and body to no other happiness but good eating and drinking,——bid him *taste and see how good God is:*——there is not an invitation in all nature would confound him like it.

In a word, a man's mind must be like your proposition, before it can be relished; and 'tis the resemblance between them, which brings over his judgment, and makes him an evidence on your side.

## SERMON VIII.

'Tis therefore not to the cruel,——'tis to the merciful;——to those who rejoice with those that rejoice, and weep with them that weep,——that we make this appeal:——'tis to the generous, the kind, the humane, that I am now to tell the sad\* story of the fatherless, and of him who hath no helper, and bespeak your almsgiving in behalf of those, who know not how to ask for it themselves.

——What can I say more?——it is a subject on which I cannot inform your judgment,——and in such an audience, I would not presume to practise upon your passions: let it suffice to say, that they whom God hath blessed with the means,——and for

\* Charity Sermon at St. Andrew's, Holborn.

whom he has done more, in bleſſing them likewiſe with a difpoſition; have abundant reaſon to be thankful to him, as the author of every good gift, for the meaſure he has beſtowed to them of both: 'tis the refuge againſt the ſtormy wind and tempeſt, which he has planted in our hearts; and the conſtant fluctuation of every thing in this world, force all the ſons and daughters of Adam to ſeek ſhelter under it by turns. Guard it by entails and ſettlements as we will, the moſt affluent plenty may be ſtripp'd, and find all its worldly comforts like ſo many withered leaves dropping from us; —the crowns of princes may be ſhaken; and the greateſt that ever awed the world, have looked back and moralized upon the turn of the wheel.

That which has happened to one, ——may happen to every man; and therefore that excellent rule of our SAVIOUR, in acts of benevolence, as well as every thing elfe, fhould govern us;——*That whatfoever ye would that men fhould do to you, do ye alfo unto them.*

Haft thou ever laid upon the bed of languifhing, or laboured under a diftemper which threatened thy life? Call to mind thy forrowful and penfive fpirit at that time, and fay, What it was that made the thoughts of death fo bitter:—if thou hadft children,——I affirm it, the bitternefs of death lay there!——if unbrought up, and unprovided for, What will become of them? Where will they find a friend when I am gone, who will ſtand up for them, and plead their cauſe againſt the wicked?

———Bleſſed God! to thee, who art a father to the fatherleſs, and a huſband to the widow,—I intruſt them.

Haſt thou ever ſuſtained any conſiderable ſhock in thy fortune? or, Has the ſcantineſs of thy condition hurried thee into great ſtraits, and brought thee almoſt to diſtraction? Conſider what was it that ſpread a table in that wilderneſs of thought,———who made thy cup to overflow? Was it not a friend of conſolation who ſtepped in, ———ſaw thee embarraſſed with tender pledges of thy love, and the partner of thy cares,——took them under his protection?——Heaven! thou wilt reward him for it!——and freed thee from all the terrifying apprehenfions of a parent's love.

——Haft thou——

——But how fhall I afk a queftion which muft bring tears into fo many eyes?—Haft thou ever been wounded in a more affecting manner ftill, by the lofs of a moft obliging friend,—or been torn away from the embraces of a dear and promifing child by the ftroke of death?——bitter remembrance! nature droops at it—but nature is the fame in all conditions and lots of life.
——A child thruft forth in an evil hour, without food, without raiment, bereft of inftruction, and the means

of its falvation, is a subject of more tender heartaches, and will awaken every power of nature:———as we have felt for ourselves,—let us feel for Christ's sake—let us feel for theirs: and may the God of all comfort bless you. Amen.

# SERMON IX.
## PRIDE.

### Luke xiv. 10, 11.

*But thou, when thou art bidden, go and sit down in the lowest room, that when he that bad thee cometh, he may say to thee, Friend, go up higher, then shalt thou have worship in the presence of them who sit at meat with thee: for whosoever exalteth himself, shall be abased; and he that humbleth himself, shall be exalted.*

IT is an exhortation of our Saviour's to Humility, addressed by way of inference from what he had said in the three foregoing verses of the chapter; where, upon entering into the house of one of the chief Pharisees to eat bread, and marking how small a portion of this necessary virtue entered in with the several guests, discovering itself from their choosing the chief rooms, and most distinguished places of honour;—he takes the occasion which such a behaviour offered, to caution them against Pride;—states the inconvenience of the passion;——shews the disappointments which attend it;——the disgrace in which it generally ends; in being forced at last to recede from the pretensions to what is more than our due; which, by the way, is the very thing the passion is eternally prompting us to expect. When, therefore, thou art bidden to a wedding, says our Saviour, sit not down in the highest room, lest a more honourable man than thou be bidden of him; and he that bad thee and him, come and say to thee,——Give this man place: and thou begin with shame to take the lowest room.

——But thou, when thou art bidden, go and sit down in the lowest room:——hard lecture!—— In the lowest room?——What,—do I owe nothing to myself? Must I forget my station, my character in life? Resign the precedence which my birth, my fortune, my talents, have already placed me in possession of?——give all up! and suffer inferiors to take my honour? Yes;——for that, says our Saviour, is the road to it: *For when he that bad thee cometh, he will say to thee, Friend, go up higher; then shalt thou have worship in the presence of them who sit at meat with thee:— for whosoever exalteth himself, shall be abased; and he that humbleth himself, shall be exalted.*

To make good the truth of which declaration, it is not necessary we should look beyond this life, and say, That in that day of retribution, wherein every high thing shall be brought low, and every irregular passion dealt with as it deserves;——that Pride, amongst the rest, (considered as a vicious character) shall meet with its proper punishment of being abased, and lying down for ever in shame and dishonour.——It is not necessary we should look so far forwards for the accomplishment of this: the words seem not so much to imply the threat of a distant punishment, the execution of which was to be respited to that day;——as the declaration of a plain truth depending upon the natural course of things, and evidently verified in every hour's commerce of the world; from whence, as well as from our reasoning upon the point, it is found, That Pride lays us open to so many mortifying encounters, which Humility in its own nature rests secure from,——that verily, each of them, in this world, have their reward faithfully dealt out by the natural workings of men's passions; which, tho' very bad executioners in general, yet are so far just ones in this, that they seldom suffer the exultations of an infolent temper to escape the abasement, or the deportment of a humble one to fail of the honour, which each of their characters do deserve.

In other vicious excesses which a man commits, the world (tho' it is not much to its credit) seems to stand pretty neuter: if you are extravagant or intemperate, you are looked upon as the greatest enemy to yourself,——— or if an enemy to the public,———at least, you are so remote a one to each individual, that no one feels himself immediately concerned in your punishment: but in the instances of Pride, the attack is personal: for as this passion can only take its rise from a secret comparison, which the party has been making of himself to my disadvantage, every intimation he gives me of what he thinks of the matter, is so far a direct injury, either as it withholds the respect which is my due,——or perhaps denies me to have any; or else, which presses equally hard, as it puts me in mind of the defects which I really have, and of which I am truly conscious, and consequently think myself the less deserving of an admonition: in every one of which cases, the proud man, in whatever language he speaks it,——if it is expressive of this superiority over me, either in the gifts of fortune, the advantages of birth or improvements, as it has proceeded from a mean estimation, and possibly a very unfair one, of the like pretenſions in myſelf,——the attack, I ſay, is perſonal; and has generally the fate to be felt and reſented as ſuch.

So that with regard to the preſent inconveniencies, there is ſcarce any vice, bating ſuch as are immediately puniſhed by laws, which a man may not indulge with more ſafety to himſelf, than this one of Pride;——the humbleſt of men, not being ſo entirely void of the paſſion themſelves, but that they ſuffer ſo much from the overflowings of it in others, as to make the literal accompliſhment of the text a common intereſt and concern: in which they are generally ſucceſsful,— the nature of the vice being ſuch, as not only to tempt you to it, but to

## SERMON IX.

afford the occasions itself of its own humiliation.

The proud man,——see!——he is sore all over; touch him——you put him to pain: and tho' of all others, he acts as if every mortal was void of all sense and feeling, yet is possessed with so nice and exquisite a one himself, that the slights, the little neglects and instances of disesteem, which would be scarce felt by another man, are perpetually wounding him, and oft-times piercing him to his very heart.

I would not therefore be a proud man, was it only for this, that it should not be in the power of every one who thought fit—to chastise me;——my other infirmities, however unworthy of me, at least will not incommode me :——so little discountenance do I see given to them, that it is not the world's fault, if I suffer by them :——but here——if I exalt myself, I have no prospect of escaping;—— with this vice I stand swoln up in every body's way, and must unavoidably be thrust back: whichever way I turn, whatever step I take under the direction of this passion, I press unkindly upon some one, and in return, must prepare myself for such mortifying repulses, as will bring me down, and make me go on my way sorrowing.

This is from the nature of things, and the experience of life as far back as Solomon, whose observation upon it was the same,——and it will ever hold good, *that before honour was humility, and a haughty spirit before a fall.* ——*Put not therefore thyself forth in the presence of the king, and stand not in the place of great men:*——*for better is it*——(which by the way is the very diffuasive in the text)——*better is it, that it be said unto thee, Friend, come up higher, than that thou shouldest be put lower in the presence of the prince whom thine eyes have seen.*

Thus much for the illustration of this one argument of our Saviour's, against Pride:——there are many other considerations which expose the weakness of it, which his knowledge of the heart of man might have suggested; but as the particular occasion which gave rise to this lecture of our

Saviour's against Pride, naturally led him to speak of the mortifications which attend such instances of it, as he then beheld:——for this reason the other arguments might be omitted, which perhaps in a set discourse would be doing injustice to the subject. I shall therefore, in the remaining part of this, beg leave to offer some other considerations of a moral as well as a religious nature upon this subject, as so many inducements to check this weak passion in man; which, tho' one of the most convenient of his infirmities,—the most painful and discourteous to society, yet, by a sad fatality, so it is, that there are few vices, except such whose temptations are immediately seated in our natures, to which there is so general a propensity throughout the whole race.

This had led some satirical pens to write, That all mankind at the bottom were proud alike;——that one man differed from another, not so much in the different portions which he possessed of it, as in the different art and address by which he excels in the management and disguise of it to the world: we trample, no doubt, too often, upon the pride of Plato's mantle, with as great a pride of our own; yet on the whole the remark has more spleen than truth in it; there being thousands, (if any evidence is to be allowed) of the most unaffected humility, and truest poverty of spirit, which actions can give proof of. Notwithstanding this, so much may be allowed to the observation, That Pride is a vice which grows up in society so insensibly;——steals in unobserved upon the heart upon so many occasions;—forms itself upon such strange pretensions, and when it has done, veils itself under such a variety of unsuspected appearances,—sometimes even under that of Humility itself;—in all which cases, Self-love, like a false friend, instead of checking, most treacherously feeds this humour,——points out some excellence in every soul to make him vain, and think more highly of himself, than he ought to think;——that, upon the whole, there is no one weakness into which the heart of man is more easily betray'd

## SERMON IX.

—— or which requires greater helps of good sense and good principles to guard against.

And first, the root from which it springs, is no inconsiderable discredit to the fruit.

If you look into the best moral writers, who have taken pains to search into the grounds of this passion,—— they will tell you, that Pride is the vice of little and contracted souls;—that whatever affectation of greatness it generally wears and carries in the looks, there is always meanness in the heart of it:——a haughty and an abject temper, I believe, are much nearer a-kin than they will acknowledge;——like *poor* relations, they look a little shy at one another at first fight, but trace back their pedigree, they are but collateral branches from the same stem; and there is scarce any one who has not seen many such instances of it, as one of our poets alludes to, in that admirable stroke he has given of this affinity, in his description of a *Pride which licks the dust*.

As it has *meanness* at the bottom of it,—so it is justly charged with having *weakness* there too, of which it gives the strongest proof, in regard to the chief end it has in view, and the absurd means it takes to bring it about.

Consider a moment,——What is it the proud man aims at?——Why, —such a measure of respect and deference, as is due to his superior merit, &c. &c.

## SERMON IX.

Now, good sense and a knowledge of the world shew us, that how much soever of these are due to a man, allowing he has made a right calculation,——they are still dues of such a nature, that they are not to be insisted upon: Honour and Respect must be a *Free-will offering:* treat them otherwise, and claim them from the world as a tax,——they are sure to be withheld; the first discovery of such an expectation disappoints it, and prejudices your title to it for ever.

To this speculative argument of its weakness, it has generally the ill fate to add another of a more substantial nature, which is matter of fact; that to turn giddy upon every little exaltation, is experienced to be no less a mark of a *weak brain* in the figurative, than it is in the literal sense of the expression——in sober truth, 'tis but a scurvy kind of a trick (*quoties voluit Fortuna jocari*)—when Fortune in one of her merry moods, takes a poor devil with this passion in his head, and mounts him up all at once as high as she can get him——for it is sure to make him play such phantastick tricks, as to become the very fool of the comedy; and was he not a general benefactor to the world in making it merry, I know not how Spleen could be pacified during the representation.

A third argument against Pride is the natural connexion it has with vices of an unsocial aspect: the Scripture seldom introduces it alone——Anger, or Strife, or Revenge, or some inimical passion, is ever upon the stage with it; the proofs and reasons of which I have not time to enlarge on, and therefore shall say no more upon this argument than this,——that was there no other,——yet the bad company this vice is generally found in, would be sufficient by itself to engage a man to avoid it.

Thus much for the moral considerations upon this subject; a great part of which, as they illustrate chiefly the inconveniencies of Pride in a social light, may seem to have a greater tendency to make men guard the appearances of it, than conquer the passion itself, and root it out of their nature: to do this effectually, we must add the arguments of religion, without which, the best moral discourse may prove little better than a cold political lecture, taught merely to govern the passion so, as not to be injurious to a man's present interest or quiet; all which a man may learn to practise well enough, and yet at the same time be a perfect stranger to the best part of humility, which implies not a concealment of Pride, but an absolute conquest over the first risings of it which are felt in the heart of man.

And, first, one of the most persuasive arguments which religion offers to this end, is that which rises from the state and condition of ourselves, both as to our natural and moral imperfections. It is impossible to reflect a moment upon this hint, but with a heart full of the humble exclamation, *O God! what is man!*——*even a thing of nought*——a poor, infirm, miserable, short-lived creature, that passes away like a shadow, and is hastening off the stage where the theatrical titles and distinctions, and the whole mask of Pride which he has worn for a day will fall off, and leave him naked as a neglected slave. Send forth your imagination, I beseech you, to view the last scene of the greatest and proudest who ever awed and governed the world—see the empty vapour disappearing! one of the arrows of mortality this moment sticks fast within him:

see—it forces out his life, and freezes his blood and spirits.

——Approach his bed of state——lift up the curtain——regard a moment with silence——

——are these cold hands and pale lips, all that is left of him who was canoniz'd by his own pride, or made a god of, by his flatterers?

O my soul! with what dreams hast thou been bewitched? how hast thou been deluded by the objects thou hast so eagerly grasped at?

If this reflection from the natural imperfection of man, which he cannot remedy, does neverthelefs strike a damp upon human Pride, much more must the considerations do so, which arise from the wilful depravations of his nature.

Survey yourselves, my dear Christians, a few moments in this light—behold a disobedient, ungrateful, intractable, and disorderly set of creatures, going wrong seven times in a day,——acting sometimes every hour of it against your own convictions—your own interests, and the intentions of your GOD, who wills and proposes nothing but your happiness and prosperity——what reason does this view furnish you for Pride? how many does it suggest to mortify and make you ashamed?——well might the son of Syrach say in that sarcastical remark of his upon it, *That* PRIDE *was not made for man*——for some purposes, and for some particular beings, the passion might have been shaped——but not for him——fancy it where you will, 'tis no where so improper—'tis in no creature so unbecoming—

——But why so cold an assent to so incontested a truth?——Perhaps thou hast reasons to be proud:——for heaven's sake, let us hear them——Thou hast the advantages of birth and title to boast of——or thou standest in the sunshine of court favour——or thou hast a large fortune——or great talents——or much learning—or nature has bestowed her graces upon thy person——speak—on which of these foundations hast thou raised this fanciful structure?——Let us examine them.

Thou art well born;——then trust me, 'twill pollute no one drop of thy blood to be humble: humility calls no man down from his rank,——divests not princes of their titles; it is in life what the *clear obscure* is in painting; it makes the hero step forth in the canvas, and detaches his figure from the group in which he would otherwise stand confounded for ever.

If thou art rich——then shew the greatness of thy fortune——or what is better, the greatness of thy soul in the meekness of thy conversation; condescend to men of low estate,——support the distressed, and patronize the neglected.——Be great; but let it be in considering riches as they are; as *talents committed to an earthen vessel—*

That thou art but the *receiver*,—and that to be obliged and be vain too,— is but the old folecifm of pride and beggary, which, tho' they often meet, ———yet ever make but an abfurd fociety.

If thou art powerful in intereft, and ftandeth deified by a fervile tribe of dependents,———why fhouldeft thou be proud,———becaufe they are hungry? —Scourge me fuch fycophants; they have turned the heads of thoufands as well as thine———

———But 'tis thy own dexterity and ftrength which have gained thee this eminence:———allow it; but art thou proud, that thou ftandeft in a place where thou art the mark of one man's envy, another man's malice, or a third man's revenge,——where good men may be ready to suspect thee, and whence bad men will be ready to pull thee down. I would be proud of nothing that is uncertain: Haman was so, because he was admitted alone to queen Esther's banquet; and the distinction raised him,——but it was fifty cubits higher than he ever dream'd or thought of.

Let us pass on to the pretences of learning, &c. &c. If thou haft a little, thou wilt be proud of it in course: if thou haft much, and good sense along with it, there will be no reason to dispute against the passion: a beggarly parade of remnants is but a sorry object of Pride at the best;——but more so, when we can cry out upon it, as the poor man did of his hatchet, ——* *Alas; Master,——for it was borrowed.*

It is treason to say the same of Beauty,——whatever we do of the arts and ornaments with which Pride is wont to set it off: the weakest minds are most caught with both; being ever glad to win attention and credit from small and slender accidents, thro' disability of purchasing them by better means. In truth, Beauty has so many charms, one knows not how to speak against it; and when it happens that a graceful figure is the habitation of a virtuous soul,—when the beauty

---

* 2 Kings, vi. 7.

of the face speaks out the modesty and humility of the mind, and the justness of the proportion raises our thoughts up to the art and wisdom of the great Creator,—something may be allowed it,——and something to the embellishments which set it off;—and yet, when the whole apology is read,——it will be found at last, that Beauty, like Truth, never is so glorious as when it goes the plainest.

Simplicity is the great friend to nature, and if I would be proud of any thing in this silly world, it should be of this honest alliance.

Consider what has been said; and may the God of all mercies and kindness watch over your passions, and inspire you *with all humbleness of mind, meekness, patience, and long suffering.*—Amen.

# SERMON X.

## Humility.

MATTHEW xi. 29.

*Learn of me, for I am meek and lowly in heart; and ye shall find rest unto your souls.*

THE great business of man, is the regulation of his spirit; the possession of such a frame and temper of mind, as will lead us peaceably through this world, and in the many weary stages of it, afford us, what we shall be sure to stand in need of,——— *Rest unto our souls.*———

———Rest unto our souls!———'tis all we want—the end of all our wishes and pursuits: give us a prospect of this, we take the wings of the morning, and fly to the uttermost parts of the earth to have it in possession: we seek for it in titles, in riches and pleasures,—climb up after it by ambition, ———come down again and stoop for it by avarice,———try all extremes; still we are gone out of the way, nor is it, till after many miserable experiments, that we are convinced at last, we have been seeking every where for it, but where there was a prospect of finding it; and that is, within ourselves, in a meek and lowly disposition of heart. This, and this only, will give us rest unto our souls:———rest, from those turbulent and haughty passions which disturb our quiet:———

## SERMON X.

rest, from the provocations and disappointments of the world, and a train of untold evils too long to be recounted, against all which this frame and preparation of mind is the best protection.

I beg you will go along with me in this argument. Consider how great a share of the uneasinesses which take up and torment our thoughts, owe their rise to nothing else, but the dispositions of mind which are opposite to this character.

With regard to the provocations and offences, which are unavoidably happening to a man in his commerce with the world,———take it as a rule, ———as a man's pride is,———so is always his displeasure;———as the opinion of himself rises,——so does the injury,——so does his resentment: 'tis this which gives edge and force to the instrument which has struck him,—— and excites that heat in the wound, which renders it incurable.

See how different the case is with the humble man: one half of these painful conflicts he actually escapes; the other part fall lightly on him:— he provokes no man by contempt; thrusts himself forward as the mark of no man's envy; so that he cuts off the first fretful occasions of the greatest part of these evils; and for those in which the passions of others would involve him, like the humble shrub in the valley, gently gives way, and scarce feels the injury of those stormy encounters which rend the proud cedar, and tear it up by its roots.

If you confider it, with regard to the many difappointments of this life, which arife from the hopes of bettering our condition, and advancing in the world,—the reafoning is the fame.

What we expect——is ever in proportion to the eftimate made of ourfelves; when pride and felf-love have brought us in their account of this matter,——we find, that we are worthy of all honours—fit for all places and employments:——as our expectations rife and multiply, fo muft our difappointments with them; and there needs nothing more, to lay the foundation of our unhappinefs, and both to make and keep us miferable. And in truth there is nothing so common in life as to see thousands, whom you would say, had all the reason in the world to be at rest, so torn up and disquieted with sorrows of this class, and so incessantly tortured with the disappointments which their pride and passions have created for them, that tho' they appear to have all the ingredients of happiness in their hands,——they can neither compound or use them:—How should they? the goad is ever in their sides, and so hurries them on from one expectation to another, as to leave them no rest day or night.

Humility, therefore, recommends itself as a security against these heart-aches, which tho' ridiculous sometimes in the eye of the beholder, yet are serious enough to the man who suffers them; and I believe would make no inconsiderable account in a true catalogue of the disquietudes of mortal man: against these, I say, Humility is the best defence.

He that is little in his own eyes, is little too in his desires, and consequently moderate in his pursuit of them: like another man, he may fail in his attempts and lose the point he aimed at,——but that is all,——he loses not himself,——he loses not his happiness and peace of mind with it,——even the contentions of the humble man are mild and placid.——Blessed character! when such a one is thrust back, who does not pity him?—when he falls, who would not stretch out a hand to raise him up?

And here, I cannot help stopping in the midst of this argument, to make a short observation, which is this. When we reflect upon the character of Humility,——we are apt to think it stands the most naked and defenceless of all virtues whatever,——the least able to support its claims against the insolent antagonist who seems ready to bear him down, and all opposition which such a temper can make.

Now, if we consider him as standing alone,—no doubt, in such a case he will be overpowered and trampled upon by his opposer;——but if we consider the meek and lowly man, as he is—fenced and guarded by the love, the friendship and wishes of all mankind,———that the other stands alone, hated, discountenanced, without one true friend or hearty well-wisher on his side;——when this is balanced, we shall have reason to change our opinion, and be convinced that the humble man, strengthened with such an alliance, is far from being so overmatched as at first sight he may appear; —nay I believe one might venture to go further and engage for it, that in all such cases, where real fortitude and true personal courage were wanted, he is much more likely to give proof of it, and I would sooner look for it in such a temper than in that of his adversary. Pride may make a man violent,———but Humility will make him firm:———and which of the two, do you think, likely to come off with honour?———he, who acts from the changeable impulse of heated blood, and follows the uncertain motions of his pride and fury,———or the man who stands cool and collected in himself; who governs his resentments, instead of being governed by them, and on every occasion acts upon the steady motives of principle and duty.

But this by the way;———though in truth it falls in with the main argument; for if the observation is just, and Humility has the advantages where we should least expect them, the argument rises higher in behalf of those which are more apparently on its side.

——In all which, if the humble man finds, what the proud man must never hope for in this world,——that is, *rest to his soul*,——so does he likewise meet with it from the influence such a temper has upon his condition under the evils of his life, not as chargeable upon the vices of men, but as the portion of his inheritance, by the appointment of God. For if, as Job says, we are born to trouble as the sparks fly upwards, surely it is he who thinks the greatest of these troubles below his sins,—and the smallest favours above his merit, that is likely to suffer the least from the one, and enjoy the most from the other: 'tis he who possesses his soul in meekness, and keeps it subjected to all the issues of fortune, that is the farthest out of their reach.——No.——He blames not the sun, though it does not ripen his vine, nor blusters at the winds, though they bring him no profit.——If the fountain of the humble man rises not as high as he could wish——he thinks however, that it rises as high as it ought, and as the laws of nature still do their duty, that he has no cause to complain against them.

If disappointed of riches—he knows the providence of God is not his debtor; that though he has received less than others, yet as he thinks himself less than the least, he has reason to be thankful.

If the world goes untoward with the humble man, in other respects,—he knows a truth which the proud man does never acknowledge, and that is, that the world was not made for him; and therefore how little share soever he has of its advantages, he sees an argument of content, in reflecting how little it is, that a compound of sin, of ignorance, and frailty, has grounds to expect.

A soul thus turned and resigned, is carried smoothly down the stream of providence; no temptations in his passage disquiet him with desire,———no dangers alarm him with fear: though open to all the changes and chances of others,———yet by seeing the justice of what happens,—and humbly giving way to the blow,———though he is smitten, he is not smitten like other men, or feels the smart which they do.

Thus much for the doctrine of Humility; let us now look towards the example of it.

It is observed by some one, that as pride was the passion through which sin and misery entered into the world, and gave our enemy the triumph of ruining our nature, that therefore the Son of God, who came to seek and to save that which was lost, when he entered upon the work of our restoration, he began at the very point where he knew we had failed; and this he did by endeavouring to bring the soul of man back to its original temper of Humility: so that his first publick address from the Mount began with a declaration of blessedness to the poor in spirit,———and almost his last exhortation in the text, was to copy the fair original he had set them of this virtue, and *to learn of him to be meek and lowly in heart.*

It is the most unanswerable appeal that can be made to the heart of man, —— and so persuasive and accommodated to all Christians, that as much pride as there is still in the world, it is not credible but that every believer must receive some tincture of the character or bias towards it from the example of so great, and yet so humble a Master, whose whole course of life was a particular lecture to this one virtue; and in every instance of it shewed, that he came not to share the pride and glories of life, or swell the hopes of ambitious followers, but to cast a damp upon them for ever, by appearing himself rather as a servant than a master,———coming, as he continually declared, not to be ministred unto, but to minister; and as the Prophet had foretold in that mournful description of him,———to have no form, or comeliness, nor any beauty that they should desire him. The voluntary meanness of his birth,———the poverty of his life,———the low offices in which it was engaged, in preaching the Gospel to the poor,—the inconveniences which attended the execution of it, in having no where to lay his head,——— all spoke the same language;———that the GOD of truth should submit to the suspicion of an imposture:—his humble deportment under that, and a thousand provocations of a thankless people, still raises this character higher;—and what exalts it to its highest pitch,——the tender and pathetick proof he gave of the same disposition at the conclusion and great catastrophe of his sufferings,—when a life full of so many instances of humility was crowned with the most endearing one of *humbling himself even to the death of the cross* ;—the death of a slave,——a malefactor——drag'd to *Calvary*, without opposition——insulted without complaint.——

—Blessed Jesus! how can the man who calls upon thy name, but learn of thee to be meek and lowly in heart?—how can he but profit when such a lesson was seconded—by such an example?

If humility shines so bright in the character of CHRIST, so does it in that of his religion; the true spirit of which tends all the same way.—Christianity, when rightly explained and practised, is all meekness and candour, and love and courtesy: and there is no one passion our SAVIOUR rebukes so often, or with so much sharpness, as that one, which is subversive of these kind effects,——and that is pride, which in proportion as it governs us, necessarily leads us on to a discourteous opinion and treatment of others.——I say *necessarily*,——because 'tis a natural consequence, and the progress from the one to the other is unavoidable.

## SERMON X.

This our Saviour often remarks in the character of the Pharisees:—— they trusted in themselves,——'twas no wonder then they despised others.

This, I believe, might principally relate to spiritual pride, which, by the way, is the worst of all prides; and as it is a very bad species of a very bad passion, I cannot do better than conclude the discourse with some remarks upon it.

In most conceits of a religious superiority, there has usually gone hand in hand with it, another fancy,—— which——I suppose has fed it;—— and that is, a persuasion of some more than ordinary aids and illuminations from above.——Let us examine this matter.

That the influence and assistance of GOD's spirit in a way imperceptible to us, does enable us to render him an acceptable service, we learn from scripture—In what particular manner this is effected, so that the act shall still be imputed ours——the scripture says not: we know only the account is so; but as for any sensible demonstrations of its workings to be felt as such within us——the word of GOD is utterly silent; nor can that silence be supplied by any experience.——We have none; unless you call the false pretences to it such,——suggested by an enthusiastic or distempered fancy. As expresly as we are told and pray for the inspiration of GOD's spirit,— there are no boundaries fixed, nor can any be ever marked to diſtinguiſh them from the efforts and determinations of our own reaſon: and as firmly as moſt Chriſtians believe the effects of them upon their hearts, I may venture to affirm, that ſince the promiſes were made, there never was a Chriſtian of a cool head and ſound judgment, that, in any inſtance of a change of life, would preſume to ſay, which part of his reformation was owing to divine help,——or which to the operations of his own mind; or who, upon looking back, would pretend to ſtrike the line, and ſay, " here " it was that my own reflections " ended;"——and at this point the ſuggeſtions of the ſpirit of God began to take place.

However backwards the world has been in former ages in the discovery of such points as GOD never meant us to know,——we have been more successful in our own days:——thousands can trace out now the impressions of this divine intercourse in themselves, from the first moment they received it, and with such distinct intelligence of its progress and workings, as to require no evidence of its truth.

It must be owned, that the present age has not altogether the honour of this discovery;—there were too many grounds given to improve on in the religious cant of the last century;—when the *in-comings, in-dwellings,* and *out-lettings* of the Spirit, were the subjects of so much edification; and, when, as they do now, the most illiterate mechanics, who, as a witty divine said of them, were much fitter to *make* a pulpit, than get into one,—were yet able so to frame their nonsense to the nonsense of the times, as to beget an opinion in their followers, not only that they pray'd and preach'd by inspiration, but that the most common actions of their lives were set about in the Spirit of the Lord.

The tenets of the quakers (a harmless quiet people) are collateral descendents from the same enthusiastic original; and their accounts and way of reasoning upon their inward light and spiritual worship, are much the fame; which last they carry thus much further, as to believe the Holy Ghost comes down upon their assemblies, and *moves* them, without regard to condition or sex, to make intercessions with unutterable groans.———

So that, in fact, the opinions of methodists, upon which I was first entering, is but a republication with some alterations of the same extravagant conceits; and as enthusiasm generally speaks the same language in all ages, 'tis but too sadly verified in this; for tho' we have not yet got to the old terms of the in-comings and in-dwellings of the spirit,———yet we have arrived at the first feelings of its enterance, recorded with as particular an exactness, as an act of filiation,———

so that numbers will tell you the identical place——the day of the month, and the hour of the night, when the spirit came in upon them, and took possession of their hearts.

Now there is this inconvenience on our side, That there is no arguing with a frenzy of this kind; for unless a representation of the case be a confutation of its folly to them, they must for ever be led captive by a delusion, from which no reasoner can redeem them: for if you should inquire, upon what evidence so strange a persuasion is grounded?——they will tell you, "They feel it is so."——If you reply, That this is no conviction to you, who do not feel it like them, and therefore would wish to be satisfied by what tokens they are able to diftinguifh fuch emotions from thofe of fancy and complexion? they will anfwer, That the manner of it is incommunicable by human language,—but 'tis a matter of fact,———they feel its operations as plain and diftinct, as the natural fenfations of pleafure, or the pains of a diforder'd body.—And fince I have mention'd a diforder'd body, I cannot help fuggefting, that amongft the more ferious and deluded of this fect, 'tis much to be doubted whether a diforder'd body has not oft times as great a fhare in letting in thefe conceits, as a diforder'd mind.

When a poor difconfolated drooping creature is terrified from all enjoyment,—prays without ceafing till his imagination is heated,——fasts and mortifies and mopes, till his body is in as bad a plight as his mind; is it a wonder, that the mechanical disturbances and conflicts of an empty belly, interpreted by an empty head, should be mistook for workings of a different kind from what they are?——or that in such a situation, where the mind sits upon the watch for extraordinary occurrences, and the imagination is pre-engaged on its side, is it strange if every commotion should help to fix him in this malady, and make him a fitter subject for the treatment of a Physician than a Divine?

In many cases, they seem so much above the skill of either, that unless

God in his mercy rebuke this lying spirit, and call it back,——it may go on and perfuade millions into their deftruction.

# SERMON XI.

## Advantages of Christianity to the World.

**ROMANS i. 22.**

*Professing themselves to be wise, they became fools.*

THERE is no one project to which the whole race of mankind is so universally a bubble, as to that of being thought Wise; and the affectation of it is so visible, in men of all complexions, that you every day see some one or other so very solicitous to establish the character, as not to allow himself leisure to do the things which fairly win it;——expending more art and stratagem to appear so in the eyes of the world, than what would suffice to make him so in truth.

It is owing to the force of this desire, that you see in general, there is no injury touches a man so sensibly, as an insult upon his parts and capacity: tell a man of other defects, that he wants learning, industry or application,——he will hear your reproof with patience——Nay you may go further: take him in a proper season, you may tax his morals,——you may tell him he is irregular in his conduct,——passionate or revengeful in his nature—loose in his principles;—— deliver it with the gentleness of a friend,——possibly he'll not only bear

## SERMON XI.

with you,——but, if ingenuous, he will thank you for your lecture, and promise a reformation;——but hint, ——hint but at a defect in his intellectuals,——touch but that sore place, ——from that moment you are look'd upon as an enemy sent to torment him before his time, and in return may reckon upon his resentment and ill-will for ever; so that in general you will find it safer to tell a man, he is a knave than a fool,——and stand a better chance of being forgiven, for proving he has been wanting in a point of common honesty, than a point of common sense.

Strange souls that we are! as if to live well was not the greatest argument of Wisdom;——and, as if what reflected upon our morals, did not most of all reflect upon our understandings!

This, however, is a reflection we make a shift to overlook in the heat of this pursuit; and tho' we all covet this great character of Wisdom, there is scarce any point wherein we betray more folly than in our judgments concerning it; rarely bringing this precious ore either to the test or the balance; and tho' 'tis of the last consequence not to be deceived in it,—we generally take it upon trust,——seldom suspect the quality, but never the quantity of what has fallen to our lot. So that however inconsistent a man shall be in his opinions of this, and what absurd measures soever he takes in consequence of it, in the conduct of his life,—he ſtills ſpeaks comfort to his ſoul; and like Solomon, when he had leaſt pretence for it,—in the midſt of his nonſenſe will cry out and ſay,——*That all my wiſdom remaineth with me.*

Where then is wiſdom to be found? and where is the place of underſtanding?

The politicians of this world, *profeſſing themſelves wiſe,*——admit of no other claims of wiſdom but the knowledge of men and buſineſs, the underſtanding the intereſts of ſtates,——the intrigues of courts——the finding out the paſſions and weakneſſes of foreign miniſters——and turning them and all events to their country's glory and advantage.——

────Not so the little man of this world, who thinks the main point of wisdom, is to take care of himself;────to be wise in his generation;────to make use of the opportunity whilst he has it, of raising a fortune, and heraldizing a name.────Far wide is the speculative and studious man (whose office is in the clouds) from such little ideas:────Wisdom dwells with him in finding out the secrets of nature;────sounding the depths of arts and sciences;────measuring the heavens; telling the number of the stars, and calling them all by their names: so that when in our busy imaginations we have built and unbuilt again *God's stories in the heavens,*────and fancy we have found out the point whereon to fix the foundations of the earth; and in the language of the book of Job, have searched out the corner-stone thereof, we think our titles to wisdom built upon the same basis with those of our knowledge, and that they will continue for ever.

The mistake of these pretenders is shewn at large by the Apostle, in the chapter from which the text is taken, ——*Professing themselves* WISE,—— in which expression (by the way) St. Paul is thought to allude to the vanity of the Greeks and Romans, who being great encouragers of arts and learning, which they had carried to extraordinary heights, considered all other nations as *Barbarians*, in respect of themselves; and amongst whom, particularly the Greeks, the men of ſtudy and inquiry had aſſumed to themſelves, with great indecorum, the title of the Wiſe-Men.

With what parade and oſtentation ſoever this was made out, it had the fate to be attended with one of the moſt mortifying abatements which could happen to Wiſdom; and that was an ignorance of thoſe points which moſt concerned man to know.

This he ſhews from the general ſtate of the gentile world, in the great article of their miſconceptions of the Deity ——and, as wrong notions produce wrong actions,——of the duties and ſervices they owed to him, and in courſe of what they owed to one another.

## SERMON XI.

For tho', as he argues in the foregoing verses,——*The invisible things of him from the creation of the world might be clearly seen and understood, by the things that are made;*——that is,

——Tho' God, by the clearest discovery of himself, had ever laid before mankind such evident proofs of his eternal Being,——his infinite powers and perfections, so that what is to be known of his invisible nature, might all along be traced by the marks of his goodness,——and the visible frame and order of the world:——yet so utterly were they without excuse,—— that tho' they knew God, and saw his image and superscription in every part of his works,——*yet they glorified him not.*——So bad a use did they make of the powers given them for this great discovery, that instead of adoring the Being thus manifested to them, in purity and truth, they fell into the most gross and absurd delusions;——*changed the glory of the incorruptible God, into an image made like unto corruptible men,—to birds,—to four-footed beasts and creeping things;* ——*Professing themselves to be wise,— they became fools.*——All their specious wisdom was but a more glittering kind of ignorance, and ended in the most dishonourable of all mistakes,——in setting up fictitious gods, to receive the tribute of their adoration and thanks.

The fountain of religion being thus poisoned,——no wonder the stream shewed its effects, which are charged upon them in the following words, where he describes the heathen world *as full of all unrighteousness,——fornication,—covetousness,--maliciousness, ——full of murder,——envy,——debate,—-malignity,——whisperers,— backbiters,——haters of* God,—— *proud,——boasters,——inventors of evil things——disobedient to parents, ——without understanding, without natural affection,——implacable,—— unmerciful!*——God in heaven defend us from such a catalogue!

But these disorders, if fairly considered, you'll say, have in no ages arisen so much from want of light, as a want of disposition to follow the light which God has ever imparted:

that the law written in their hearts, was clear and exprefs enough for any reafonable creatures, and would have directed them, had they not fuffered their paffions more forcibly to direct them otherwife: that if we are to judge from this effect, namely, the corruption of the world, the fame prejudice will recur even againft the Chriftian religion; since mankind have at leaft been as wicked in later days, as in the more remote and fimple ages of the world; and that, if we may truft to facts, there are no vices which the Apoftle fixes upon the heathen world, before the preaching of the gofpel, which may not be paralleled by as black a catalogue of vices in the Chriftian world fince.

This necessarily brings us to an inquiry, Whether Christianity has done the world any service?——and, How far the morals of it have been made better since this system has been embraced?

In litigating this, one might oppose facts to facts to the end of the world, without coming one jot nearer the point. Let us see how far their mistakes concerning the Deity, will throw light upon the subject.

That there was one supreme Being who made this world, and who ought to be worshipped by his creatures, is the foundation of all religion, and so obvious a truth in nature,——that Reason, as the Apostle acknowledges, was always able to discover it: and yet it seems strange, that the same faculty which made the discovery, should be so little able to keep true to its own judgment, and support it long against the prejudices of wrong heads, and the propensity of weak ones, towards idolatry and a multiplicity of gods.

For want of something to have gone hand in hand with reason, and fixed the persuasion for ever upon their minds, that there was in truth but one God the Maker and Supporter of Heaven and Earth,—infinite in wisdom, and knowledge, and all perfections;——how soon was this simple idea lost, and mankind led to dispose of these attributes inherent in the Godhead, and divide and subdivide them again amongst deities, which their own dreams had given substance to;——his eternal power and dominion parcell'd out to gods of the land,——to gods of the sea,——to gods of the infernal regions; whilst the great GOD of gods, and LORD of lords, who ruleth over all the kingdoms of the world,——who is so great that nought is able to controul or withstand his power, was supposed to rest contented with his allotment, and to want power to act within such parts of his empire, as they dismembered and assigned to others.

If the number of their gods and this partition of their power, would lessen the idea of their majesty, What must be the opinions of their origin? When instead of that glorious description, which Scripture gives of "The Ancient of days who inhabiteth eternity,"——they gravely affigned particular times and places for the births and education of their gods; fo that there was fcarce a hamlet or even a defert in Greece or Italy, which was not rendered memorable by fome favour or accident of this kind.

And what rendered fuch conceits the more grofs and abfurd,——they fuppofed not only that the gods they worfhipped had a beginning, but that they were produced by flefhly parents, and accordingly, they attributed to them corporeal fhapes and difference of fex: and indeed in this they were a little confiftent, for their deities feemed to partake fo much of the frailties to which flesh and blood is subject, that their history and their pedigree were much of a piece, and might reasonably claim each other. For they imputed to them not only the human defects of ignorance, want, fear, and the like, but the most unmanly sensualities, and what would be a reproach to human nature,——such as cruelty, adulteries, rapes, incests; and even in the accounts which we have from the sublimest of their poets,——what are they, but anecdotes of their squabbles amongst themselves—their intrigues, their jealousies, their ungovernable transports of choler,—nay, even their thefts—their drunkenness, and bloodshed!

Here let us stop a moment and inquire, what was Reason doing all this time, to be so miserably insulted and abused? Where held she her empire whilst her bulwarks were thus borne down, and her first principles of religion and truth lay buried under them? If she was able by herself to regain the power she had lost, and put a stop to this folly and confusion,——why did she not? If she was not able to resist this torrent alone,—the point is given up——she wanted aid; and revelation has given it.

But tho' reason, you'll say, could not overthrow these popular mistakes, ——yet it saw the folly of them, and was at all times able to disprove them.

## SERMON XI.

No doubt it was; and it is certain too, that the more diligent inquirers after truth, did not in fact fall into these absurd notions, which, by the way, is an observation more to our purpose than theirs, who usually make it, and shews that tho' their reasonings were good, that there always wanted something which they could not supply to give them such weight, as would lay an obligation upon mankind to embrace them, and make that to be a law, which otherwise was but an opinion without force.

Besides——which is a more direct answer,——tho' 'tis true, the ablest men gave no credit to the multiplicity of gods,——(for they had a religion, for themselves, and another for the populace) yet they were guilty of what in effect was equally bad, in holding an opinion which necessarily supported these very mistakes,——namely, that as different nations had different gods, it was every man's duty (I suppose more for quietness than principle's sake) to worship the gods of his country; which, by the way, considering their numbers, was not so easy a task;——for what with celestial gods, and gods aërial, terrestrial and infernal, with the goddesses, their wives and mistresses, upon the lowest computation, the heathen world acknowledged no less than thirty thousand deities, all which claimed the rites and ceremonies of religious worship.

But, 'twill be said, allowing the bulk of mankind were under such delusions,——they were still but speculative.——What was that to their practice? however defective in their theology and more abstracted points,——their morality was no way connected with it.——There is no need, that the everlasting laws of justice and mercy should be fetched down from above,——since they can be proved from more obvious mediums;—— they were as necessary for the same good purposes of society then as now; and we may presume they saw their interest and pursued it.

That the necessities of society, and the impossibilities of its subsisting otherwise, would point out the convenience, or if you will,——the duty of social virtues, is unquestionable:—but I firmly deny, that therefore religion and morality are independent of each other: they appear so far from it, that I cannot conceive how 'the one, in the true and meritorious sense of the duty, can act without the influence of the other: surely the most exalted motive which can only be depended upon for the uniform practice of virtue,——must come down from *above*,——from the love and imitation of the goodness of that Being in whose sight we wish to render ourselves acceptable: this will operate at all times and all places,——in the darkest closet as much as on the greatest and most public theatres of the world.

## SERMON XI.

But with different conceptions of the Deity, or such impure ones as they entertained, is it to be doubted whether in the many secret trials of our virtue, we should not determine our cases of conscience with much the same kind of casuistry as that of the Libertine in Terence, who being engaged in a very unjustifiable pursuit, and happening to see a picture which represented a known story of Jupiter in a like transaction,——argued the matter thus within himself.——If the great Jupiter could not restrain his appetites, and deny himself an indulgence of this kind——*ego Homuncio hoc non facerem?* shall I a mortal,—an inconsiderable mortal too, cloath'd with infirmities of flesh and blood,—

pretend to a virtue, which the Father of gods and men could not? What insolence!

The conclusion was natural enough; and as so great a master of nature puts it into the mouth of one of his principal characters, no doubt the language was then understood; it was copied from common life, and was not the first application which had been made of the story.

It will scarce admit of a question, Whether vice would not naturally grow bold upon the credit of such an example; or whether such impressions did not influence the lives and morals of many in the heathen world; and had there been no other proof of it, but the natural tendency of such no-

## SERMON XI.

tions to corrupt them, it had been sufficient reason to believe it was so?

No doubt, there is sufficient room for amendment in the christian world, and we may be said to be a very corrupt and bad generation of men, considering what motives we have from the purity of our religion, and the force of its sanctions, to make us better:——yet still I affirm, if these restraints were taken off, the world would be infinitely worse: and tho' some sense of morality might be preserved, as it was in the heathen world, with the more considerate of us, yet in general I am persuaded, that the bulk of mankind, upon such a supposition, would soon come to *live without* GOD *in the world*, and in a short time differ from Indians themselves in little else but their complexions.

If after all, the christian religion has not left a sufficient provision against the wickedness of the world,——the short and true answer is this, That there can be none.

It is sufficient to leave us without excuse, that the excellency of this institution in its doctrine, its precepts, and its examples, has a proper tendency to make us a virtuous and a happy people;——every page is an address to our hearts to win them to these purposes;——but as religion was not intended to work upon men by force and natural necessity, but by moral persuasion, which sets good and evil before them,——so that if men have power to do the evil and chuse the good,——and will abuse it,—— this cannot be avoided.——Religion ever implies a freedom of choice, and all the beings in the world which have it, were created free to stand and free to fall;——and therefore men who will not be persuaded by this way of address, must expect, and be contented to be reckoned with according to the talents they have received.

## SERMON XII.

### The Abuses of Conscience considered.

Hebrews xiii. 18.

——*For we trust we have a good Conscience* ———

TRUST!——Trust we have a good Conscience!——Surely you will say, if there is any thing in this life which a man may depend upon, and to the knowledge of which he is capable of arriving upon the most indisputable evidence, it must be this very thing,———Whether he has a good Conscience, or no.

## SERMON XII.

If a man thinks, at all, he cannot well be a stranger to the true state of this account:——He must be privy to his own thoughts and desires——He must remember his past pursuits, and know certainly the true springs and motives, which, in general, have govern'd the actions of his life.

In other matters we may be deceiv'd by false appearances; and, as the wise man complains, *Hardly do we guess aright at the things that are upon the earth, and with labour do we find the things that are before us:*——but here the mind has all the evidence and facts within herself:——is conscious of the web she has wove——knows its texture and fineness, and the exact share which every passion has had in working upon the several designs, which virtue or vice has plann'd before her.

Now,——as Conscience is nothing else but the knowledge which the mind has within itself of this; and the judgment, either of approbation or censure, which it unavoidably makes upon the successive actions of our lives,——'tis plain, you will say, from the very terms of the proposition, whenever this inward testimony goes against a man, and he stands self-accused,——that he must necessarily be a *guilty man*. And, on the contrary, when the report is favourable on his side, and his heart condemns him not,——that it is not a matter of *trust*, as the Apostle intimates, but a matter of certainty and fact, that the *Conscience* is *good*, and that the *man* must be *good* also.

At first sight, this may seem to be a true state of the case; and I make no doubt but the knowledge of right and wrong is so truly impress'd upon the mind of man; that, did no such thing ever happen, as that the conscience of a man, by long habits of sin, might (as the Scripture assures us it may) insensibly become hard; and, like some tender parts of his body, by much stress, and continual hard usage, lose, by degrees, that nice sense and perception with which God and nature endowed it:——Did this never happen:—or was it certain that self-love could never hang the least bias upon the judgment:—or that the little interests below could rise up and perplex the faculties of our upper regions, and encompass them about with clouds and thick darkness:——could no such thing as favour and affection enter this sacred court:——did WIT disdain to take a bribe in it, or was ashamed to shew its face as an advocate for an unwarrantable enjoyment:—or, lastly, were we assured that INTEREST stood always unconcern'd whilst the cause was hearing,—and that PASSION never got into the judgment seat, and pronounced sentence in the stead of reason, which is supposed always to preside and determine upon the case: —was this truly so, as the objection must suppose, no doubt, then, the religious and moral state of a man would be exactly what he himself esteemed it; and the guilt or innocence of every man's life could be known, in general, by no better measure, than the degrees of his own approbation or censure.

I own, in one case, whenever a man's Conscience does accuse him (as it seldom errs on that side) that he is guilty; and, unless in melancholy and hypochondriac cases, we may safely pronounce that there is always sufficient grounds for the accusation.

But, the converse of the proposition will not hold true,——namely, That wherever there is guilt, the Conscience must accuse; and, if it does not, that a man is therefore innocent.——This is not fact:——fo that the common confolation which fome good Chriftian or other is hourly adminiftering to himfelf,——That he thanks GOD his mind does not mifgive him; and that, confequently, he has a good Confcience, becaufe he has a quiet one— As current as the inference is, and as infallible as the rule appears at firft fight, yet, when you look nearer to it, and try the truth of this rule upon plain facts, you find it liable to fo much error, from a falfe application of it:—the principle on which it goes fo often perverted:—the whole force of it loft, and fometimes fo vilely caft away, that it is painful to produce the common examples from human life, which confirm this account.

## SERMON XII.

A man shall be vicious and utterly debauched in his principles; exceptionable in his conduct to the world: shall live shameless,——in the open commission of a sin which no reason or pretence can justify;—a sin, by which, contrary to all the workings of humanity within, he shall ruin for ever the deluded partner of his guilt;——rob her of her best dowry;——and not only cover her own head with dishonour, but involve a whole virtuous family in shame and sorrow for her sake. Surely,——you'll think, conscience must lead such a man a troublesome life:——he can have no rest night or day from its reproaches.

Alas! Conscience had something else to do all this time than break in

## SERMON XII.

upon him: as *Elijah* reproached the god *Baal,* this *domestic God* was either *talking, or pursuing, or was in a journey, or, peradventure, he slept and could not be awoke.* Perhaps he was gone out in company with Honour, to fight a duel;——to pay off some debt at play;——or dirty annuity, the bargain of his lust.——Perhaps, Conscience all this time was engaged at home, talking aloud against petty larceny, and executing vengeance upon some such puny crimes as his fortune and rank in life secured him against all temptation of committing:——so that he lives as merrily,——sleeps as soundly in his bed;——and, at the last, meets death with as much unconcern,———perhaps, much more so, than a much better man.

Another is sordid, unmerciful;—a strait-hearted, selfish wretch, incapable either of private friendships, or publick spirit.——Take notice how he passes by the widow and orphan in their distress; and sees all the miseries incident to human life without a sigh or a prayer.——Shall not Conscience rise up and sting him on such occasions? No.——Thank God, there is no occasion. 'I pay every man his
' own,——I have no fornication to
' answer to my Conscience, no faith-
' less vows or promises to make up,
' I have debauch'd no man's wife or
' child.——Thank God I am not as
' other men, adulterers, unjust, or

'even as this libertine who stands
'before me.'

A third is crafty and designing in his nature.——View his whole life,——'tis nothing else but a cunning contexture of dark arts and unequitable subterfuges, basely to defeat the true intent of all laws, plain-dealing, and the safe enjoyment of our several properties——You will see such a one working out a frame of little designs upon the ignorance and perplexities of the poor and needy man:——shall raise a fortune upon the inexperience of a youth,——or the unsuspecting temper of his friend, who would have trusted him with his life. When old age comes on, and repentance calls him to look back upon this black account, and state it over again with his Conscience——Conscience looks into the *Statutes at Large*,—— finds perhaps no *express law* broken by what he has done;——perceives no penalty or forfeiture incurr'd;—— sees no scourge waving over his head, ——or prison opening its gate upon him.——What is there to affright his Conscience?——Conscience has got safely entrench'd behind the letter of the law, sits there invulnerable, fortified with *cases* and *reports* so strongly on all sides,——that 'tis not preaching can dispossess it of its hold.

Another shall want even this refuge,——shall break thro' all this ceremony of slow chicane; scorns the doubtful workings of secret plots and cautious trains to bring about his purpose.——See the bare-fac'd villain how he cheats, lyes, perjures, robs, murders,——— horrid! But indeed much better was not to be expected in this case.——The poor man was in the dark!——His priest had got the keeping of his Conscience,—and all he had let him know of it was, That he must believe in the *Pope*;— go to mass;——cross himself;——tell his beads;——be a good Catholic; and that this in all conscience was enough to carry him to heaven. What?——if he perjures?——Why, ——he had a mental reservation in it. But if he is so wicked and abandoned a wretch as you represent him, ——if he robs, or murders, will not

Conscience, on every such act, receive a wound itself?——Ay——But the man has carried it to confession, the wound digests there, and will do well enough,——and in a short time be quite healed up by absolution.

O *Popery!* what hast thou to answer for?——when not content with the too many natural and fatal ways thro' which the heart is every day thus treacherous to itself above all things,——thou hast wilfully set open this wide gate of deceit before the face of this unwary *Traveller*,——too apt, God knows, to go astray of himself,——and confidently speak peace to his soul, when there is no peace.

Of this the common instances, which I have drawn out of life, are too notorious to require much evidence. If any man doubts the reality of them, or thinks it impossible for man to be such a bubble to himself,—I must refer him a moment to his reflections, and shall then venture to trust the appeal with his own heart. Let him consider in how different a degree of detestation numbers of wicked actions stand *there*, though equally bad and vicious in their own natures—— he will soon find that such of them as strong inclination or custom have prompted him to commit, are generally dress'd out and painted with all the false beauties which a soft and a flattering hand can give them; and that the others to which he feels no propensity, appear, at once, naked and deformed, surrounded with all the true circumstances of folly and dishonour.

When David surprised Saul sleeping in the cave, and cut off the skirt of his robe,——we read, his heart smote him for what he had done.——But, in the matter of Uriah, where a faithful and gallant servant, whom he ought to have lov'd and honour'd, fell to make way for his lust; where *Conscience* had so much greater reason to take the alarm,———his heart smote him not.——A whole year had almost passed from the first commission of that crime——to the time Nathan was sent to reprove him; and we read not once of the least sorrow or compunction of heart, which he testified during all that time, for what he had done.

Thus Conscience, this once able monitor,—placed on high as a judge within us,——and intended, by our Maker, as a just and equitable one too,—by an unhappy train of causes and impediments,——takes often such imperfect cognizance of what passes,——does its office so negligently,—sometimes so corruptly, that it is not to be trusted alone: and therefore, we find, there is a necessity, an absolute necessity, of joining another principle with it, to aid, if not govern, its determinations.

So that if you would form a just judgment of what is of infinite importance to you not to be misled in, namely, in what degree of real merit you stand, either as an honest man,——an useful citizen,——a faithful subject to your king,——or a good servant to your God——call in Religion and Morality.——Look——What is written in the law of God?——How readest thou?———Consult calm reason, and the unchangeable obligations of justice and truth,——What say they?

Let Conscience determine the matter upon these reports,——and then, if *thy heart condemn thee not*,—— which is the case the Apostle supposes,——the rule will be infallible, ——*Thou wilt have confidence towards God*;——that is, have just grounds to believe the judgment thou hast past upon thyself, *is* the judgment of God; and nothing else but an anticipation of that righteous sentence, which will be pronounced, hereafter, upon thee by that Being, before whom thou art finally to give an account of thy actions.

*Blessed is the man*, indeed then, as the Author of the book of *Ecclesiasticus* expresses it, *who is not pricked with the multitude of his sins.*—*Blessed is the man whose heart hath not condemned him, and who is not fallen from his hope in the Lord. Whether he be rich*, continues he, *or whether he be poor,*——*if he have a good heart*, (a heart thus guided and inform'd) ——*He shall at all times rejoice in a cheerful countenance*——*His mind shall tell him more than seven watchmen that sit above upon a tower on high.* In the darkest doubts it shall conduct him safer than a thousand Casuists, and give the state he lives in a better security for his behaviour, than all the clauses and restrictions put together, which the wisdom of the legislature is forced to multiply,——forced, I say, as things stand; human laws being not a matter of original choice, but of pure necessity, brought in to fence against the mischievous effects of those Consciences which are no law unto themselves: wisely intending by the many provisions made, That in all such corrupt or misguided cases, where principle and the checks of Conscience will not make us upright,——to supply their force, and by the terrors of jails and halters oblige us to it.

To have the fear of God before our eyes; and, in our mutual dealings with each other, to govern our actions by the eternal measures of right and wrong:——the first of these will comprehend the duties of religion: the second those of morality: which are so inseparably connected together, that you cannot divide these two *Tables*, even in imagination (tho' the attempt is often made in practice) without breaking and mutually destroying them both.

I said the attempt is often made; ——and so it is;——there being nothing more common than to see a man, who has no sense at all of religion,——and indeed has *so much* of honesty, as to pretend to none; who would yet take it as the bitterest affront, should you but hint at a suspicion of his moral character,——or imagine he was not conscientiously just, and scrupulous to the uttermost mite.

When there is some appearance that it is so,——though one is not willing even to suspect the appearance of so great a virtue, as moral honesty;— yet were we to look into the grounds of it in the present case, I am persuaded we should find little reason to envy such a man the honour of his motive.

Let him declaim as pompously as he can on the subject, it will be found at laſt to reſt upon no better foundation than either his intereſt, his pride, his eaſe; or ſome ſuch little and changeable paſſion, as will give us but ſmall dependence upon his actions in matters of great ſtreſs.

Give me leave to illuſtrate this by an example.

I know the banker I deal with, or the phyſician I uſually call in, to be neither of them men of much religion: I hear them make a jeſt of it every day, and treat all its ſanctions with ſo much ſcorn and contempt, as to put the matter paſt doubt. Well,——notwithſtanding this I put my fortune into the hands of the one, ——and, what is dearer ſtill to me, I truſt my life to the honeſt ſkill of the other.——Now let me examine what is my reason for this great confidence.——Why,—in the first place, I believe that there is no probability that either of them will employ the power, I put into their hands, to my disadvantage. I consider that honesty serves the purposes of this life,——I know their success in the world depends upon the fairness of their character;——that they cannot hurt me without hurting themselves more.

But put it otherwise, namely, that interest lay for once on the other side.——That a case should happen wherein the one, without stain to his reputation, could secrete my fortune, and leave me naked in the world:——or that the other could send me out of it, and enjoy an eftate by my death, without difhonour to himfelf or his art——In this cafe what hold have I of either of them?—— Religion, the ftrongeft of all motives, is out of the queftion.——Intereft, the next moft powerful motive in this world, is ftrongly againft me.——I have nothing left to caft into the fcale to balance this temptation.——I muft lay at the mercy of honour,——or fome fuch capricious principle.—Strait fecurity! for two of my beft and moft valuable bleffings,——my property and my life!

As therefore we can have no dependence upon morality without religion;——fo, on the other hand, there is nothing better to be expected from religion without morality; nor can any man be supposed to discharge his duties to God, (whatever fair appearances he may hang out, that he does so) if he does not pay as conscientious a regard to the duties which he owes his fellow-creature.

This is a point capable in itself of strict demonstration.——Nevertheless, 'tis no rarity to see a man whose real moral merit stands very low, who yet entertains the highest notion of himself, in the light of a devout and religious man. He shall not only be covetous, revengeful, implacable,——but even wanting in points of common honesty.——Yet because he talks loud against the infidelity of the age,——is zealous for some points of religion,——goes twice a day to church, attends the facraments, and amufes himfelf with a few inftrumental duties of religion,———fhall cheat his confcience into a judgment that for this he is a religious man, and has difcharged faithfully his duty to God : and you will find, that fuch a man, through force of this delufion, generally looks down with fpiritual pride upon every other man who has lefs affectation of piety, tho', perhaps, ten times more moral honefty than himfelf.

*This is likewife a fore evil under the fun*; and I believe there is no one miftaken principle which, for its time, has wrought more ferious mifchiefs. For a general proof of this, examine the history of the *Romish* church.— See what scenes of cruelty, murders, rapines, bloodshed, have all been sanctified by a religion not strictly governed by morality.

In how many kingdoms of the world, has the crusading sword of this misguided Saint-Errant spared neither age, or merit, or sex, or condition.——And, as he fought under the banners of a religion, which set him loose from justice and humanity,——he shewed none,——mercilessly trampled upon both, heard neither the cries of the unfortunate, nor pitied their distresses.

If the testimony of past centuries in this matter is not sufficient,——— consider at this instant, how the vo-

## SERMON XII.

taries of that religion are every day thinking to do service and honour to GOD, by actions which are a dishonour and scandal to themselves.

To be convinced of this, go with me for a moment into the prisons of the inquisition,———Behold *religion* with mercy and justice chain'd down under her feet,——there sitting ghastly upon a black tribunal, propp'd up with racks and instruments of torment.——Hark!——What a piteous groan!——See the melancholy wretch who utter'd it, just brought forth to undergo the anguish of a mock-trial, and endure the utmost pains that a studied system of *religious cruelty* has been able to invent. Behold this helpless victim delivered up to his tormentors. His body so wasted with sorrow and long confinement, you'll see every nerve and muscle as it suffers.———Observe the last movement of that horrid engine.———What convulsions it has thrown him into.——— Consider the nature of the posture in which he now lies stretch'd———What exquisite torture he endures by it.— 'Tis all nature can bear.———Good God! see how it keeps his weary soul hanging upon his trembling lips, willing to take its leave,——— but not suffered to depart. Behold the unhappy wretch led back to his cell,———dragg'd out of it again to meet the flames,———and the insults in his last agonies, which this principle ———this principle that there can be religion without morality, has prepared for him.

The sureft way to try the merit of any difputed notion,——is to trace down the confequences fuch a notion has produced, and compare them with the *spirit* of chriftianity.——'Tis the fhort and decifive rule, which our SAVIOUR has left for thefe and fuch like cafes,——and is worth a thoufand arguments.—*By their fruits*, fays he, *ye fhall know them.*

Thus religion and morality, like faft friends and natural allies, can never be fet at variance, without the mutual ruin and difhonour of them both;——and whoever goes about this unfriendly office, is no wellwifher to either,——and whatever he pretends, he deceives his own heart, and, I fear, his morality, as well as his religion, will be vain.

I will add no farther to the length of this discourse, than by two or three short and independent Rules, deducible from what has been said.

1*st*, Whenever a man talks loudly against religion, always suspect that it is not his reason, but his passions which have got the better of his creed.—A *bad life* and a *good belief are* disagreeable and troublesome neighbours, and where they separate, depend upon it, 'tis for no other cause but quietness sake.

2*dly*, When a man thus represented, tells you in any particular instance, that such a thing goes *against* his conscience,——always believe he means exactly the same thing as when he tells you such a thing goes against his stomach,——a present want of appetite being generally the true cause of both.

In a word,——trust that man in nothing,——who has not a conscience in every thing.

And in your own case remember this plain distinction, a mistake in which has ruin'd thousands——That your conscience is not a law;—no,—God and reason made the law, and has placed Conscience within you to determine,—not like an *Asiatic Cadi*, according to the ebbs and flows of his own passions;——but like a *British judge* in this land of liberty, who makes no new law,——but faithfully declares that glorious law which he finds already written.

# SERMON XIII.

## Temporal Advantages of Religion.

PROVERBS iii. 17.

*Her ways are ways of pleasantness, and all her paths are peace.*

THERE are two opinions which the inconsiderate are apt to take upon trust.—The first is—a vicious life, is a life of liberty, pleasure, and happy advantages.—The second is—and which is the converse of the first—that a religious life is a servile and most uncomfortable state.

The first breach which the devil made upon human innocence, was by

## SERMON XIII.

the help of the firſt of theſe ſuggeſtions, when he told Eve, that by eating of the tree of knowledge, ſhe ſhould be as God, that is, ſhe ſhould reap ſome high and ſtrange felicity from doing what was forbidden her.—— But I need not repeat the ſucceſs—Eve learnt the difference between good and evil by her tranſgreſſion, which ſhe knew not before—but then ſhe fatally learnt at the ſame time, that the difference was only this—that good is that which can only give the mind pleaſure and comfort—and that evil is that, which muſt neceſſarily be attended ſooner or later with ſhame and ſorrow.

As the deceiver of mankind thus began his triumph over our race—ſo has he carried it on ever since by the very same argument of delusion.——— That is, by possessing men's minds early with great expectations of the present incomes of sin,——making them dream of wonderous gratifications they are to feel in following their appetites in a forbidden way—making them fancy, that their own grapes yield not so delicious a taste as their neighbours, and that they shall quench their thirst with more pleasure at his fountain, than at their own. This is the opinion which at first too generally prevails—till experience and proper seasons of reflection make us all at one time or other confess—that our counsellor has been (as from the beginning) an impostor——and that inſtead of fulfilling theſe hopes of gain and ſweetneſs in what is forbidden—that on the contrary, every unlawful enjoyment leads only to bitterneſs and loſs.

The ſecond opinion, or, That a religious life is a ſervile and uncomfortable ſtate, has proved a no leſs fatal and capital falſe principle in the conduct of unexperience through life—the foundation of which miſtake ariſing chiefly from this previous wrong judgment—that true happineſs and freedom lies in a man's always following his own humour—that to live by moderate and preſcrib'd rules, is to live without joy——that not to proſecute our paſſions is to be cowards—

and to forego every thing for the tedious distance of a future life.

Was it true that a virtuous man could have no pleasure but what should arise from that remote prospect——I own we are by nature so goaded on by the desire of present happiness, that was that the case, thousands would faint under the discouragement of so remote an expectation ——But in the mean time the Scriptures give us a very different prospect of this matter.—There we are told that the service of God is true liberty—that the yoke of Christianity is easy in comparison of that yoke which must be brought upon us by any other system of living,—and the text tells of wisdom—by which he means Religion, that it has pleasantness in its way, as well as glory in its end——that it will bring us peace and joy, such as the world cannot give.———So that upon examining the truth of this assertion, we shall be set right in this error, by seeing that a religious man's happiness does not stand at so tedious a distance—but is so present and indeed so inseparable from him, as to be felt and tasted every hour—and of this even the vicious can hardly be insensible, from what he may perceive to spring up in his mind, from any casual act of virtue. And tho' it is a pleasure that properly belongs to the good—yet let any one try the experiment, and he will see what is meant by that, moral delight, arising from the conscience of well-doing.—Let him but refresh the bowels of the needy—let him comfort the broken-hearted—or check an appetite, or overcome a temptation—or receive an affront with temper and meekness—and he shall find the tacit praise of what he has done, darting thro' his mind, accompanied with a sincere pleasure—conscience playing the monitor even to the loose and most inconsiderate, in their most casual acts of well-doing, and is, like a voice whispering behind and saying—this is the way of pleasantness—this is the path of peace—walk in it.—

But to do further justice to the text, we must look beyond this inward recompence which is always inseparable from virtue——and take a view of the outward advantages, which are as inseparable from it, and which the Apostle particularly refers to, when 'tis said, Godliness has the promise of this life, as well as that which is to come—and in this argument it is, that religion appears in all its glory and strength—unanswerable in all its obligations——that besides the principal work which it does for us in securing our future well-being in the other world, it is likewise the most effectual means to promote our present——and that not only *morally*, upon account of that reward which virtuous actions do entitle a man unto from a just and a wise providence,—but by a natural tendency in themselves, which the duties of religion have *to procure* us riches, health, reputation, credit, and all those things, wherein our temporal happiness is thought to consist,—and this not only in promoting the well-being of particular persons, but of public communities and of mankind in general,——agreeable to what the wise man has left us on record, that righteousness exalteth a nation:—insomuch,—that could we, in considering this argument, suppose ourselves to be in a capacity of expostulating with God, concerning the terms upon which we would submit to his government,——and to chuse the laws ourselves which we would be bound to obferve, it would be impoffible for the wit of man to frame any other propofals, which upon all accounts would be more advantageous to our own interefts than thofe very conditions to which we are obliged by the rules of religion and virtue.——And in this does the reafonablenefs of chriftianity, and the beauty and wifdom of providence, appear moft eminently towards mankind, in governing us by fuch laws as do moft apparently tend to make us happy,——and in a word, in making that (in his mercy) to be our duty, which in his wifdom he knows to be our intereft,—that is to fay, what is moft conducive to the eafe and comfort of our mind,—the health and ftrength of our body,— the honour and profperity of our ftate and condition,—the friendfhip and good-will of our fellow-creatures;—to the attainment of all which, no more effectual means can possibly be made use of, than that plain direction,—to lead an uncorrupted life, and to do the thing which is right, to use no deceit in our tongue, nor do evil to our neighbour.

For the better imprinting of which truth in your memories, give me leave to offer a few things to your confideration.

The first is,—that justice and honesty contribute very much towards all the faculties of the mind: I mean, that it clears up the understanding from that mist, which dark and crooked designs are apt to raise in it,—and that it keeps up a regularity in the affections, by suffering no lusts or *by-ends* to disorder them.—That it likewise preserves the mind from all damps of grief and melancholy, which are the sure consequences of unjust actions; and that by such an improvement of the faculties, it makes a man so much the abler to discern, and so much the more chearful, active and diligent to mind his business.—Light is sown for the righteous, says the prophet, and gladness for the upright in heart.

Secondly, let it be observed,—that in the continuance and course of a virtuous man's affairs, there is little probability of his falling into considerable disappointments or calamities;—not only because guarded by the providence of God, but that honesty is in its own nature the freeſt from danger.

Firſt, becauſe ſuch a one lays no projects, which it is the intereſt of another to blaſt, and therefore needs no indirect methods or deceitful practices to ſecure his intereſt by undermining others.—The paths of virtue are plain and ſtraight, ſo that the blind, perſons of the meaneſt capacity, ſhall not err.—Diſhoneſty requires ſkill to conduct it, and as great art to conceal—what 'tis every one's intereſt to detect. And I think I need not remind you how oft it happens in attempts of this kind—where worldly men, in haſte to be rich, have overrun the only means to it,—and for want of laying their contrivances with proper cunning, or managing them with proper secrecy and advantage, have lost for ever, what they might have certainly secured by honesty and plain-dealing.—The general causes of the disappointments in their business, or of unhappiness in their lives, lying but too manifestly in their own disorderly passions, which by attempting to carry them a shorter way to riches and honour, disappoint them of both for ever, and make plain their ruin is from themselves, and that they eat the fruits, which their own hands have watered and ripened.

Consider, in the third place, that as the religious and moral man (one of which he cannot be without the other) not only takes the surest course for success in his affairs, but is disposed to procure a help, which never enters into the thoughts of a wicked one: for being conscious of upright intentions, he can look towards heaven, and with some assurance recommend his affairs to God's blessing and direction:———whereas the fraudulent and dishonest Man, dares not call for God's blessing upon his designs,—or, if he does, he knows it is in vain to expect it.—Now a man who believes that he has God on his side, acts with another sort of life and courage, than he who knows he stands alone;—like Esau, with his hand against every man, and every man's hand against his.

The eyes of the Lord are upon the righteous, and his ears are open to their cry,—but the face of the Lord is against them that do evil.

Consider, in the fourth place, that in all good governments who understand their own interest, the upright and honest man stands much fairer for preferment, and much more likely to be employed in all things when fidelity is wanted:—for all men, however the case stands with themselves, they love at least to find honesty in those they trust; nor is there any usage we more hardly digest, than that of being outwitted and deceived.—This is so true an observation, that the greatest knaves have no other way to get into business, but by counterfeiting honesty, and pretending to be what they are not; and when the imposture is discovered, as it is a thousand to one but it will, I have just said, what must be the certain consequence:—for when such a one falls,—he has none to help him,—so he seldom rises again.——

This brings us to a fifth particular, in vindication of the text,—That a virtuous man has this strong advantage on his side (the reverse of the last) that the more and the longer he is known, so much the better is he loved,—so much the more trusted;—so that his reputation and his fortune have a gradual increase:—and if calamities or cross accidents should bear him down,—(as no one ſtands out of their reach in this world)—— if he ſhould fall, who would not pity his diſtreſs,—who would not ſtretch forth his hand to raiſe him from the ground!——wherever 'there was virtue, he might expect to meet a friend and brother.—And this is not merely ſpeculation, but fact, confirmed by numberleſs examples in life, of men falling into misfortunes, whoſe character and tried probity have raiſed them helps, and bore them up, when every other help has forſook them.

Laſtly, to ſum up the account of the temporal advantages which probity has on its ſide,—let us not forget that greatest of all happiness, which the text refers to,—in the expression of all its paths being peace,—peace and content of mind, arising from the consciousness of virtue, which is the true and only foundation of all earthly satisfaction; and where that is wanting, whatever other enjoyments you bestow upon a wicked man, they will as soon add a cubit to his stature as to his happiness.—In the midst of the highest entertainments,——this, like the hand-writing upon the wall, will be enough to spoil and disrelish the feast;—but much more so, when the tumult and hurry of delight is over,—when all is still and silent,—when the sinner has nothing to do but attend its lashes and remorses;—and this, in spite of all the common arts of diversion, will be often the case of every wicked man;—for we cannot live always upon the stretch;—our faculties will not bear constant pleasure any more than constant pain;——there will be some vacancies; and when there are, they will be sure to be filled with uncomfortable thoughts and black reflections.—So that, setting aside the great after-reckoning, the pleasures of the wicked are overbought, even in this world.—

I conclude with one observation upon the whole of this argument, which is this.——

Notwithstanding the great force with which it has been often urged by good writers,—there are many cases which it may not reach,—wherein vicious men may seem to enjoy their portion of this life,—and live as happy, and fall into as few troubles as other men:—and, therefore, it is prudent not to lay more stress upon this argument than it will bear:—but always remember to call into our aid, that great and more unanswerable argument, which will answer the most doubtful cases which can be stated,—and that is, certainty of a future life, which christianity has brought to light. However men may differ in their opinions of the usefulness of virtue for our present purposes,—no one was ever so absurd, as to deny it served our best and our laſt intereſt,—when the little intereſts of this life were at an end:—upon which conſideration we ſhould always lay the great weight which it is fitteſt to bear, as the ſtrongeſt appeal, and moſt unchangeable motive that can govern our actions at all times.—However, as every good argument on the ſide of religion ſhould in proper times be made uſe of,—it is fit ſometimes to examine this,—by proving virtue is not even deſtitute of a preſent reward,—but carries in her hand a ſufficient recompence for all the ſelf-denials ſhe may occaſion:—ſhe is pleaſant in the way,—as well as in the end;—her ways being ways of pleaſantneſs, and all her paths peace. —But it is her greateſt and moſt di·

stinguished glory,—that she befriends us hereafter, and brings us peace at the last;—and this is a portion she can never be disinherited of,—which may God of his mercy grant us all, for the sake of Jesus Christ.

## SERMON XIV.

Our Converſation in Heaven.

PHILIPPIANS iii. 20. 1ſt Part.

*For our converſation is in Heaven.*

THESE words are the concluſion of the account which St. Paul renders of himſelf, to juſtify that particular part of his conduct and proceeding,—his leaving ſo ſtrangely, and deſerting his Jewiſh rites and ceremonies, to which he was known to have been formerly ſo much attached, and in defence of which he had been ſo warmly and ſo remarkably engaged. This, as it had been matter of provocation against him amongst his own countrymen the Jews, so was it no less an occasion of surprise to the Gentiles;—that a person of his great character, interest and reputation,—one who was descended from a tribe of Israel, deeply skilled in the professions, and zealous in the *observances of the straitest sect of that religion*; who had their tenets instilled into him from his tender years, under the institution of the ablest masters;—a Pharisee himself,—the son of a Pharisee, and brought up at the feet of Gamaliel,—one that was so deeply interested, and an accessary in the persecution of another religion, just then newly come up;—a religion to which his whole sect, as well as himself, had been always the bitterest and most inveterate enemies, and were constantly upbraided as such, by the first founder of it;—that a person so beset, and hem'd in with interests and prejudices on all sides, should after all turn proselyte to the very religion he had hated;—a religion too, under the most universal contempt of any then in the world,—the chiefs and leaders of it men of the lowest birth and education, without any advantages of parts or learning, or other endowments to recommend them:—that he should quit and abandon all his former privileges, to become merely a fellow-labourer with these,—that he should give up the reputation he had acquired amongst his brethren by the study and labours of a whole life;——that he should give up his friends,—his relations and family, from whom he estranged and banished himself for life; ——this was an event so very extraordinary,—so odd and unaccountable,—that it might well confound the minds of men to answer for it.——It was not to be accounted for upon the common rules and measures of proceeding in human life.——

The Apostle, therefore, since no one else could so well do it for him, comes, in this chapter, to give an explanation why he had thus forsaken so many worldly advantages,—which was owing to a greater and more unconquerable affection to a better and more valuable interest, that in the poor perſecuted faith,—which he had once reproached and deſtroyed,—he had now found ſuch a fullneſs of divine grace,——ſuch unfathomable depths of God's infinite mercy, and love towards mankind, that he could think nothing too much to part with in order to his embracing Chriſtianity;—nay, he accounted all things but loſs,—that is, leſs than nothing, for the excellency of the knowledge of Jeſus Chriſt.

The Apoſtle, after this apology for himſelf,—proceeds, in the ſecond verſe before the text, to give a very different repreſentation of the worldly views and ſenſual principles of other pretending teachers,——who had ſet themſelves up as an example for men to walk by, againſt whom he renews this caution :——For many walk, of whom I have told you often, and now tell you even weeping, that they are the enemies to the croſs of Chriſt,—whoſe end is deſtruction,—whoſe God is their belly, and whoſe glory is in their ſhame, who mind earthly things,—Φρωνϑῖες,—reliſh them, making them the only object of their wiſhes,—taking aim at nothing better, and nothing higher.——But *our* converſation, ſays he in the text, is in heaven.—We chriſtians, who have embraced a perſecuted faith, are governed by other conſiderations,—— have greater and nobler views;—here we conſider ourſelves only as pilgrims and ſtrangers.—Our home is in another country, where we are continually tending; there our hearts and affections are placed; and when the few days of our pilgrimage shall be over, there shall we return, where a quiet habitation and a perpetual rest is designed and prepared for us for ever.— Our conversation is in heaven, from whence, says he, we also look for the Saviour, the Lord Jesus Christ, who shall change our vile body, that it may be fashioned like unto his glorious body, according to the working whereby he is able to subdue all things unto him.—It is observable, that St. Peter represents the state of christians under the same image, of strangers on earth, whose city and proper home, is heaven:—he makes use of that relation of citizens of heaven, as a strong argument for a pure and holy life,—beseeching them *as* pilgrims and strangers *here*, as men whose interests and connexions are of so short a date, and so trifling a nature,——to abstain from fleshly lusts, which war against the soul, that is, unfit it for its heavenly country, and give it a disrelish to the enjoyment of that pure and spiritualized happiness, of which that region must consist, wherein there shall in no wise enter any thing that defileth, neither whatsoever worketh abomination.— The apostle tells us, that without holiness no man shall see God;—by which no doubt he means, that a virtuous life is the only medium of happiness and terms of salvation,—which can only give us admission into heaven.——But some of our divines carry the assertion further, that without holiness,—without some previous similitude wrought in the faculties of the mind, corresponding with the nature of the purest of beings, who is to be the object of our fruition hereafter;——that it is not morally only, but physically impossible for it to be happy,——and that an impure and polluted soul, is not only unworthy of so pure a presence as the spirit of God, but even incapable of enjoying it, could it be admitted.

And here, not to feign a long hypothesis, as some have done, of a sinner's being admitted into heaven, with a particular description of his condition and behaviour there,—we need only consider, that the supreme good, like any other good, is of a relative nature, and consequently the enjoyment of it must require some qualification in the faculty, as well as the enjoyment of any other good does;—there must be something antecedent in the disposition and temper, which will render that good a good to that individual,——otherwise though (it is true) it may be possessed,—yet it never can be enjoyed.—

Preach to a voluptuous epicure, who knows of no other happiness in this world, but what arises from good eating and drinking;—such a one, in the apostle's language, whose God was his belly;—preach to him of the abstractions of the soul, tell of its flights, and brisker motion in the pure regions of immensity;—represent to him that saints and angels eat not,—but that the spirit of a man lives for ever upon wisdom and holiness, and heavenly contemplations:—why, the only effect would be, that the fat glutton would stare a while upon the preacher, and in a few minutes fall fast asleep.—No; if you would catch his attention, and make him take in your discourse greedily,—you must preach to him out of the Alcoran,—talk of the raptures of sensual enjoyments, and of the pleasures of the perpetual feasting, which Mahomet has described;—there you touch upon a note which awakens and sinks into the inmost recesses of his soul;—without which, discourse as wisely and abstractedly as you will of heaven, your representations of it, however glorious and exalted, will pass like the songs of melody over an ear incapable of discerning the distinction of sounds.—

We see, even in the common intercourses of society,—how tedious it is to be in the company of a person whose humour is disagreeable to our own, though perhaps in all other respects of the greatest worth and excellency.—How then can we imagine that an ill-disposed soul, whose conversation never reached to heaven, but whose appetites and desires, to the last hour, have grovel'd upon this unclean spot of earth;——how can we imagine it should hereafter take pleasure in God, or be able to taste joy or satisfaction from his presence, who is so infinitely pure, that he even putteth no trust in his saints,——nor are the heavens themselves (as Job says) clean in his sight.—The consideration of this has led some writers so far, as to say, with some degree of irreverence in the expression,——that it was not in the power of God to make a wicked man happy, if the soul was separated from the body, with all its vicious habits and inclinations unreformed;—

which thought, a very able divine in our church has pursued so far, as to declare his belief,——that could the happiest mansion in heaven be supposed to be allotted to a gross and polluted spirit, it would be so far from being happy in it, that it would do penance there to all eternity:—— by which he meant, it would carry such appetites along with it, for which there could be found no suitable objects.—A sufficient cause for constant torment;—for those that it found there, would be so disproportioned, that they would rather vex and upbraid it, than satisfy its wants.— This, it is true, is mere speculation,— and what concerns us not to know;— it being enough for our purpose, that such an experiment is never likely to be tried,—that we stand upon different terms with God,——that a virtuous life is the foundation of all our happiness,—that as God has no pleasure in wickedness, neither shall any evil dwell with him;—and that, if we expect our happiness to be in heaven,—we must have our conversation in heaven, whilst upon earth, make it the frequent subject of our thoughts and meditations,—let every step we take tend that way,—every action of our lives be conducted by that great mark of the prize of our high-calling, forgetting those things which are behind;——forgetting this world,—disengaging our thoughts and affections from it, and thereby transfforming them to the likeness of what we hope to be hereafter.—How can we expect the inheritance of the saints of light, upon other terms than what they themselves obtained it?——

Can that body expect to rise and shine in glory, that is a slave to lust, or dies in the fiery pursuit of an impure desire? Can that heart ever become the lightsome seat of peace and joy, that burns hot as an oven with anger, rage, envy, lust, and strife? full of wicked imaginations, set only to devise and entertain evil?

Can that flesh appear in the last day, and inherit the kingdom of heaven in the glorified strength of perpetual youth, that is now clearly confumed in intemperance, finks in the furfeit of continual drunkennefs and gluttony, and then tumbles into the grave, and almoft pollutes the ground that is under it?—Can we reafonably fuppofe, that head fhall ever wear or become the crown of righteoufnefs and peace, in which dwells nothing but craft and avarice, deceit and fraud and treachery,——which is always plodding upon worldly defigns, racked with ambition,—rent afunder with difcord,——ever delighting in mifchief to others, and unjuft advantages to itfelf;—Shall that tongue, which is the glory of a man when rightly directed,—be ever fet to God's heavenly praifes, and warble forth the harmonies of the blessed, that is now full of cursing and bitterness, backbiting and slander, under which is ungodliness and vanity and the poison of asps?

Can it enter into our hearts even to hope, that those hands can ever receive the reward of righteousness, that are full of blood, laden with the wages of iniquity, of theft, rapine violence, extortion, or other unlawful gain? or that those feet shall ever be beautiful upon the mountains of light and joy, that were never shod for the preparation of the gospel,—that have run quite out of the way of God's word,——and made haste only to do evil?—No surely.—In this sense,—he that is unjust, let him be unjuft ftill, and he which is filthy, let him be filthy ftill.

How inconfiftent the whole body of fin is, with the glories of the celeftial body that fhall be revealed hereafter,——and that in proportion as we fix the reprefentation of thefe glories upon our minds, and in the more numerous particulars we do it,—the ftronger the neceffity as well as perfuafion to deny ourfelves all ungodlinefs and worldly lufts, to live foberly, righteoufly and godly in this prefent world, as the only way to entitle us to that bleffednefs fpoken of in the Revelations—of thofe who do his commandments, and have a right to the tree of life, and fhall enter into the gates of the city of the living God, the heavenly Jerufalem, and to an innumerable company of angels;——to the general affembly and church of the firſt-born, that are written in heaven, and to God the judge of all, and to the ſpirits of juſt men made perfect,—who have waſhed their robes, and made them white in the blood of the Lamb.——

May God give us grace to live under the perpetual influence of this expectation,——that by the habitual impreſſion of theſe glories upon our imaginations, and the frequent ſending forth our thoughts and employing them on the other world,——we may diſentangle them from this,—— and by ſo having our converſation in heaven whilst we are here, we may be thought fit inhabitants for it hereafter;—that when God at the last day shall come with thousands and ten thousands of his saints to judge the world, we may enter with them into happiness, and with angels and arch-angels, and all the company of heaven, we may praise and magnify his glorious name, and enjoy his presence for ever.

END OF THE FOURTH VOLUME.

# BIBLIOLIFE

## Old Books Deserve a New Life
www.bibliolife.com

Did you know that you can get most of our titles in our trademark **EasyScript**™ print format? **EasyScript**™ provides readers with a larger than average typeface, for a reading experience that's easier on the eyes.

Did you know that we have an ever-growing collection of books in many languages?

Order online:
www.bibliolife.com/store

Or to exclusively browse our **EasyScript**™ collection:
www.bibliogrande.com

At BiblioLife, we aim to make knowledge more accessible by making thousands of titles available to you – quickly and affordably.

Contact us:
BiblioLife
PO Box 21206
Charleston, SC 29413